GHARIAL VS. SLOTH BEAR

BY NATHAN SOMMER

BELLWETHER MEDIA • MINNEAPOLIS, MN

Torque brims with excitement perfect for thrill-seekers of all kinds. Discover daring survival skills, explore uncharted worlds, and marvel at mighty engines and extreme sports. In *Torque* books, anything can happen. Are you ready?

This edition first published in 2025 by Bellwether Media, Inc.

No part of this publication may be reproduced in whole or in part without written permission of the publisher.
For information regarding permission, write to Bellwether Media, Inc.,
Attention: Permissions Department,
6012 Blue Circle Drive, Minnetonka, MN 55343.

Library of Congress Cataloging-in-Publication Data

LC record for Gharial vs. Sloth Bear available at:
https://lccn.loc.gov/2024019775

Editor: Suzane Nguyen   Designer: Hunter Demmin

Printed in the United States of America, North Mankato, MN.

TABLE OF CONTENTS

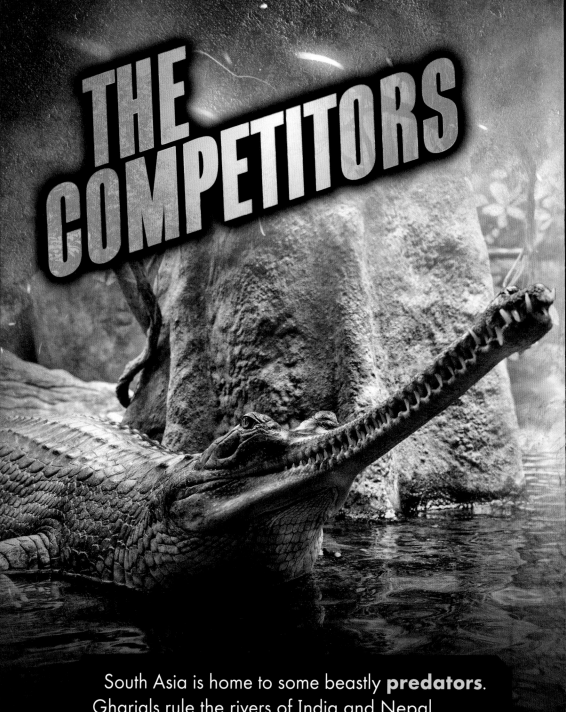

THE COMPETITORS

South Asia is home to some beastly **predators**. Gharials rule the rivers of India and Nepal. They use deadly bites to feast on **prey**.

Sloth bears grunt and snort through forests. These bears are dangerous to those who come too close. What happens when these animals face off?

Gharials are large **reptiles**. They grow to 15 feet (4.6 meters) long. They weigh around 400 pounds (181.4 kilograms). These reptiles have long, thin **snouts**. They have strong bodies with short legs.

Male gharials have a bump on their snouts called a ghara. They use their ghara to make sounds. The sounds help them find **mates**.

GHARA

RARE REPTILES

Gharials are critically endangered in the wild.

GHARIAL PROFILE

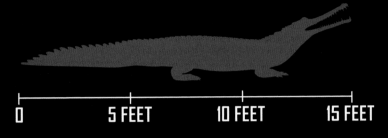

0   5 FEET   10 FEET   15 FEET

LENGTH
AROUND 15 FEET
(4.6 METERS)

WEIGHT
AROUND 400 POUNDS
(181.4 KILOGRAMS)

HABITAT

FRESHWATER
RIVERS

GHARIAL RANGE

☐ RANGE

SLOTH BEAR PROFILE

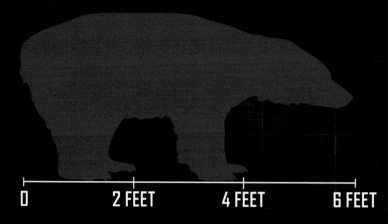

0   2 FEET   4 FEET   6 FEET

LENGTH
UP TO 6 FEET
(1.8 METERS)

WEIGHT
UP TO 310 POUNDS
(141 KILOGRAMS)

HABITATS

FORESTS   GRASSLANDS

SLOTH BEAR RANGE

☐ RANGE

Sloth bears are one of South Asia's most dangerous **mammals**. They are **solitary** animals that roam forests and grasslands at night.

Sloth bears have long snouts. They have dark, shaggy fur with white chest markings. These bears grow up to 6 feet (1.8 meters) long. They weigh up to 310 pounds (141 kilograms).

SECRET WEAPONS

Strong, flat tails and webbed feet make gharials **agile** swimmers. They **propel** themselves through water. This helps them easily catch fish.

SLOTH BEAR CLAW

**3 INCHES
(7.6 CENTIMETERS)**

Sloth bear claws grow up to 3 inches (7.6 centimeters) long. Their curved claws help them rip through rock-hard termite mounds. They also use their claws as weapons against enemies.

Gharials have up to 110 razor-sharp teeth. Their teeth fit together to hold onto slippery fish. Prey often cannot escape the gharials' deadly **grip**.

NUMBER OF TEETH

GHARIAL = 110 TEETH
x10 x10 x10 x10 x10 x10 x10 x10 x10 x10 x10

ALLIGATOR = 80 TEETH
x10 x10 x10 x10 x10 x10 x10 x10

Sloth bears have large **canine teeth**. They have two each on their top and bottom jaws. The bears use their canines to hurt enemies.

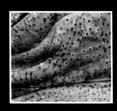

STRONG, FLAT TAIL   RAZOR-SHARP TEETH   SENSORS

Gharials have tiny **sensors** in their scales and snouts. These find the movements of prey underwater. The reptiles can easily find their food.

SECRET WEAPONS

CURVED CLAWS   LARGE CANINE TEETH   STRONG SENSE OF SMELL

Sloth bears have a strong sense of smell.
They sometimes stand on their hind legs to smell
the air. They can smell if predators are near.

ATTACK MOVES

Gharials are quiet hunters. They often float completely still in water and wait for prey. Then, they quickly strike as prey swim by.

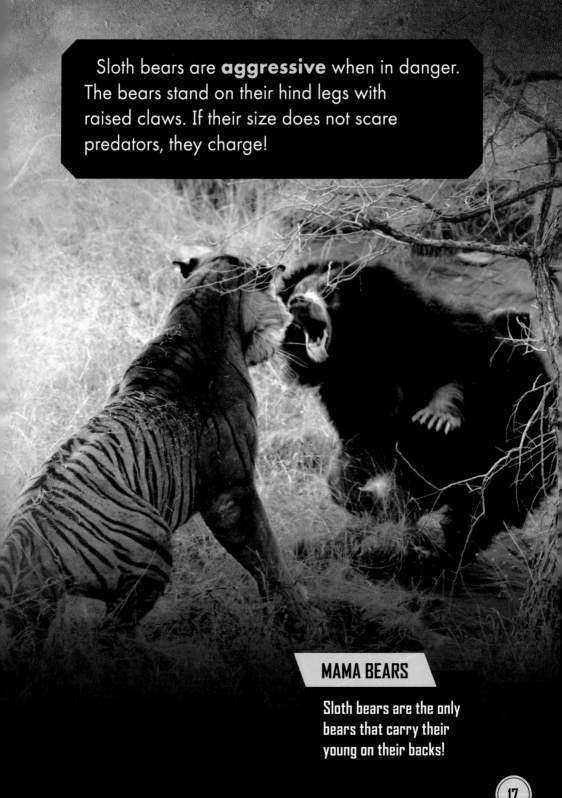

Sloth bears are **aggressive** when in danger. The bears stand on their hind legs with raised claws. If their size does not scare predators, they charge!

MAMA BEARS

Sloth bears are the only bears that carry their young on their backs!

Gharials use sensors in their snouts to hunt.
They move their heads back and forth to find prey.
Then, they quickly snatch their meal with their jaws.

Sloth bears make loud sucking noises when eating. These sounds can be heard from 330 feet (101 meters) away!

Sloth bears attack their enemies with powerful claws. They slash the heads and necks of predators. They deliver painful bites with their sharp canine teeth.

READY, FIGHT!

A gharial suns itself in shallow water. It scares a sloth bear walking by. This causes the bear to charge! It bites the gharial.

The gharial bites back! It sinks its razor-sharp teeth into the bear's arm. The gharial escapes into deeper water. The hurt bear runs away. The speedy reptile avoids a deadly attack today!

GLOSSARY

aggressive—ready to fight

agile—able to move quickly and easily

canine teeth—long, pointed teeth that are often the sharpest in the mouth

grip—a tight hold

mammals—warm-blooded animals that have backbones and feed their young milk

mates—partners to produce offspring

predators—animals that hunt other animals for food

prey—animals that are hunted by other animals for food

propel—to push forward quickly

reptiles—cold-blooded animals that have backbones and lay eggs

sensors—body parts that sense movement, heat, light, or sound

snouts—the nose and mouth areas on some animals

solitary—related to living alone

TO LEARN MORE

AT THE LIBRARY

Downs, Kieran. *Nile Crocodile vs. Hippopotamus*. Minneapolis, Minn.: Bellwether Media, 2022.

Gunasekara, Mignonne, and Charis Mather. *Ruthless Reptiles*. Minneapolis, Minn.: Bearport Publishing, 2024.

Sommer, Nathan. *Burmese Python vs. Sun Bear*. Minneapolis, Minn.: Bellwether Media, 2024.

ON THE WEB

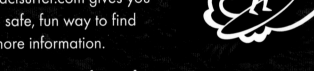

FACTSURFER

Factsurfer.com gives you a safe, fun way to find more information.

1. Go to www.factsurfer.com

2. Enter "gharial vs. sloth bear" into the search box and click 🔍.

3. Select your book cover to see a list of related web sites.

INDEX